AROUND
HAYWARDS
HEATH
IN OLD PHOTOGRAPHS

Caught Courting at
Hayward's Heath.

A CHARMING POSTCARD sent in 1909. The lady has pink flowers on her hat and carries a red parasol.

AROUND
HAYWARDS
HEATH
IN OLD PHOTOGRAPHS

COLLECTED BY
JUDY MIDDLETON

Judy Middleton

Alan Sutton Publishing Limited
Gloucester

First published 1989

British Library Cataloguing in Publication Data

Haywards Heath in old photographs.
1. West Sussex. Haywards Heath, history
I. Middleton, Judy
942.2'65

ISBN 0-86299-607-4

Typesetting and origination by
Alan Sutton Publishing Limited.
Printed in Great Britain by
Dotesios Printers Limited.

CONTENTS

THE BOATHOUSE at Buxshalls, Lindfield, captured on a languid Edwardian afternoon by F. Douglas Miller.

INTRODUCTION

Haywards Heath has been curiously neglected as regards books on local history. The number of publications could not even be dignified with the word handful. In fact Haywards Heath has been something of a Sussex Cinderella.

It may be that the neglect has been due to its proximity to some of the loveliest of Sussex villages. There is Lindfield whose High Street even stern critics like Nairn and Pevsner admit to be, 'without any doubt the finest village street in East Sussex.' Then there is the charm of Cuckfield close by and not far away beautifully situated Ditchling. In the general rush to admire these villages, Haywards Heath is forgotten or at best there might be a brief nod in passing towards the church of St Wilfrid.

However, Haywards Heath is worthy of notice, especially when you consider it was virtually a Victorian creation and we all know that in the swings and roundabouts of fashion, Victorian life and values are currently at the top of the tree. One might add Victorian industry too, since the two aspects of Haywards Heath with which everyone is familiar are the railway and the hospital of St Francis – both marvellous monuments to Victorian muscle.

It is interesting to reflect that Haywards Heath was not originally included in the route of the London to Brighton railway. The line was planned to pass through Cuckfield, but the good inhabitants of that place, or rather the wealthy landowners, were so horrified at the prospect that they brought pressure to bear in high places and Cuckfield was left in peace. At that time Haywards Heath was a small place, probably not differing much from 1800 when there were only about 20 houses altogether, of which two were inns and eight were farmhouses. The irony was that although Haywards Heath burgeoned as a result of the railway, it still remained part of Cuckfield parish and in fact did not achieve independent civil parish status until 1894.

The railway reached as far south as Haywards Heath by July 1841. Already constructed on the way was one of the marvels of the line, the Balcombe viaduct stretching across the Ouse valley near Ardingly on 37 graceful arches. Passengers travelled to Haywards Heath by train and then on to Brighton by coach and horses until the rest of the line was finished. The first through train ran on 21 September 1841, which is a remarkable achievement when you think of the major obstacle that the digging of Clayton tunnel presented, and that the whole line was completed in three years. Haywards Heath was literally on the map.

Five years after the opening of the line, a group of Justices was deliberating upon the necessity of building an asylum for pauper lunatics in East Sussex. It is nice to know that they were thinking about the problem before an Act of Parliament in 1854 made it compulsory. It was decided that it would be more practical to build one asylum for the whole county and as Haywards Heath was practically in the middle of the county and on the railway line too, it seemed the best choice. The spot selected was actually in Wivelsfield and it was situated on a ridge with wide views and plenty of healthy air. The authorities were delighted.

The architect selected for the project was Henry Edward Kendall junior whose design was deemed to be the most eligible, as well as being the least expensive of the plans submitted by four top architects. The result is a truly magnificent yellow brick structure with polychrome decorations. The scale of the building is breathtaking and to complete the picture there is a chapel nearby with an Italianate tower. It seems a pity that a question mark should hang over a complex of such character.

It should be stressed that the instigators of this hospital never envisaged it as being a dumping ground for hopeless cases (and they had to battle with the various workhouse guardians over this) but as a refuge where cures might be effected. As the patients came from poverty stricken backgrounds, the benefits of clean surroundings, good food and sympathetic help did indeed work wonders.

The hospital was remarkably self-contained as it had its own farm, pumping station, brewery, bakery, laundry – not to mention its own workforce of bricklayers, glaziers and painters plus artisans such as tailors, shoemakers, mat makers and basket makers to teach the patients.

Music has always been part of the St Francis tradition and it is interesting to note that earlier in this century no male attendant was engaged unless he could play an instrument or was good at sport, preferably both.

The church of St Wilfrid is well sited and its tower is visible in many of the old photographs used in this book. It was designed by G.F. Bodley and built in 1863–65, at a cost of £6,000, in local sandstone of a mellow shade. Unfortunately, some of the early postcards have coloured it a most unpleasant yellow.

Haywards Heath also attracted two large Roman Catholic foundations. They were the Holy Cross Convent established at Bolnore Road in the 1870s and the Priory of Our Lady of Good Counsel in Hazelgrove Road built in the 1880s.

The Priory was intended as a school for the education of girls of the higher classes. This brings us on to another important fact – the great flourishing of private schools at Haywards Heath. In fact it seems to have taken over from Hove and other seaside resorts where so many private schools had been established. Pressure on land forced many to move. One that did move was Brunswick, the boys' prep. school formerly in Oathall Road. Tradition relates that this was originally the Misses Thompson's School in Brunswick Place, Hove, which was attended by Winston Churchill in the 1880s. There was also Holland House School which started off in Hove and removed to Burgess Hill in the 1920s and is now known as St Peter's Court.

A private girls' school of note was Farlington, next door to Brunswick in Oathall Road. It was founded in 1896 by Miss Isabel Moberly whose aunt Miss Anne Moberly was one of the two famous ladies who saw the ghosts at Versailles. It is remarkable that there were only two headmistresses during the 59 years Farlington remained at Haywards Heath. Miss Moberly was head until 1942 and Miss Effie Simpson was head from 1942 until 1971 (the school moved to Horsham in 1955). Farlington stood in 12 acres of grounds which included its own private wood and stream, a hard tennis court, five grass tennis courts, besides an orchard and a huge field for lacrosse. Trevelyan was another well-known girls' school situated in Church Road. It closed down in 1966. Both of these schools were primarily boarding schools and attendance at St Wilfrid's for morning service on Sundays was compulsory. The vicar had a crowded church without trying. There was a sea of blue (the colour of Trevelyan's uniform) and pews of bottle green (the Farlington colour).

There were other private schools as well but all these have passed into history and estates of new houses have crept over the playing fields.

Independent of the self-contained existence of these large institutions, the ordinary life of Haywards Heath was flourishing. Although the streets look remarkably empty to our eyes, the shops and small businesses were bustling and if any unusual event occurred there were people to witness it faster than the photographer could make it from his premises. This book then, is a nostalgic look at Haywards Heath in bygone years.

SECTION ONE

Shops

ARTHUR PRATT'S BUTCHER'S SHOP in Sussex Road in around 1910. The boy sitting on the pig is Dick Pratt who was given 6d. to sit there and smile. Afterwards he rushed off and spent it all on lemonade dabs and got a ticking off from his mother.

URIDGE THE GROCER was established in 1878 at Sussex Square. Gladys Uridge's grandmother stands on the front step.

JUST ABOUT ANYTHING was sold in Beeny's Emporium in Sydney Road as it was the largest shop in the area. Note the window full of straw boaters.

MR PRATT also had another butcher's shop. This one occupied Aberdeen House in South Road.

R. S. BURSTOW,

 . . THE MID-SUSSEX . .
TOBACCO and CIGAR STORES,

SOUTH ROAD (Opposite the Public Hall),

HAYWARDS HEATH.

Finest Selection of **Tobaccos, Cigars, Cigarettes and Tobacconists' Fancy Goods** at London Prices.

Hairdressing and Shaving. By an Experienced London Hand.

A GUIDE BOOK to Haywards Heath printed in around 1910 contained this and the following three advertisements.

J. W. Avery,

Fulling Mill Dairy Farm

and

South Road Creamery,

HAYWARDS HEATH.

PURE NEW MILK from Jersey Cows.
High-class BUTTER.
. New-laid Eggs fresh daily. .
CREAM fresh daily and entirely free
from preservatives.

A Trial respectfully solicited.

41

THE OLD FASHIONED MILKING STOOL is still being put to good use in this photograph, whereas the selling of preservative-free cream is right up to date.

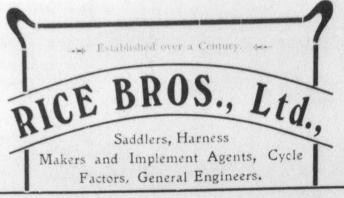

THE RICE BROTHERS certainly catered for a wide public, from horse riders to bicyclists and motorists.

MR PIPER'S SHOP had a gleaming counter and chairs for the comfort of his customers. Note also that he was selling Spey Royal Whisky for 4s.

THE INTERNATIONAL STORES in South Road in around 1914. From left to right: ? Hollingdale, Lily Shore (Thorpe), Lily Blunt (Kent), Miss Crowther, Mr Nutt (Manager), Alice Murrell, Reg Goddard and Leslie Carey.

THE SCAYNES HILL BAKERY run by J.J. Luckens in around 1910. Note the patriarchal figure on the left.

MR J.W. UPTON pictured outside his shop at the top of the Broadway in 1913. His window blind carried the wording 'Ancient and Modern Furniture'.

MR JIM DINNAGE (on the left) standing outside his cycle shop in the 1930s. Later he branched out into the motor business.

AN EXHIBITION in the Public Hall extolling the benefits of gas cooking in June 1933. There were 140 entries in the cake making competition.

A SPLENDIDLY DATED ADVERTISEMENT from 1932 featuring a Haywards Heath commuter whose servant problem was solved by the acquisition of a new gas fire.

MR AVERY'S SHOP in Wivelsfield Green served as a post office, grocer and draper. The photograph dates from around 1910.

WILLIAM KENWARD, sub-postmaster, stands in front of the Wivelsfield Post Office in around 1903. Mr Kenward was also sexton, parish clerk, school attendance officer and harness maker.

SECTION TWO

Streets

A MARVELLOUS TURN-OUT of the local children enhances this view of Gower Road taken in around 1912.

ASHENGROUND ROAD photographed in around 1912. The house on the right, on the corner of Gower Road, is called Zoylands.

Sussex Square, Hayward's Heath

A DESERTED LOOKING SUSSEX SQUARE in around 1912. The carriage on the left has stopped outside Uridge the grocer while Selby the chemist has his blind drawn down.

SUSSEX ROAD in around 1905. The building on the right was known as the Primitive Methodist Church and was built in 1877.

JAMES BOX'S SHOP was so well-known that the slope leading down into Wivelsfield Road was nicknamed Box's Hill. James Box was a butcher and his shop also sold provisions, china and glass.

WIVELSFIELD ROAD in around 1906. The sign on the white house reads 'H. Barnes Furniture Remover.' Henry Barnes had competition because Samuel Barnes was also in business as a furniture remover in the same road.

THIS VIEW of Little Haywards Road was posted in 1906.

HAYWARDS ROAD was once called Little Haywards Road after the farm of that name. However, the residents did not feel the 'little' added any lustre to their address so it was dropped.

A NOSTALGIC VIEW of South Road. This postcard is one of a series printed in around 1913 in colour with an oval border of olive green.

THIS POSTCARD carries the wrong caption. It should read South Road. There are not many postcards showing such a rain drenched view.

The Broadway.   Hayward's Heath.

THE BROADWAY in around 1907. A solitary lady stands in front of South of England Dairies. Other Broadway shops of 1907 were: Broadley Brothers (tailors), Kate Guilbert (stationer), A.D. Street (grocer), Ben Stott (draper) and Archie Taylor (boot dealer).

Broadway, Haywards Heath

A SUMMERTIME VIEW of the Broadway dating from around 1913.

COMMERCIAL SQUARE in around 1905, showing Beeny's shop on the right and Bricknell (pork butcher) and W. Holman (grocer) on the left.

BOLTRO ROAD in around 1906. The buildings on the right are the Cuckfield Rural District Council Offices (demolished in the 1980s).

A POSTCARD featuring Oathall Road photographed by H. Tullet and posted in 1906.

LOOKING SOUTH along Mill Green Road in around 1912. Note St Wilfrid's on the horizon and the gasometer on the right. Gasworks had been sited beside the railway since 1866.

AN INTERESTING OLD VIEW taken from the top of St Wilfrid's Church. Note the Star public house in the centre and the triangular-shaped Muster Green beyond it.

A VIEW OF HAYWARDS HEATH taken from Rocky Lane with St Wilfrid's visible on the left.

Houses, Farms and Other Buildings

ST CLAIR was one of Haywards Heath's grand residences. Later it was occupied by a girls' school founded in the 1930s by Miss Stevens.

POPULARLY CALLED DICK TURPIN'S COTTAGE, this old dwelling was demolished when a police station was built on the site in 1887.

IT MUST HAVE BEEN HIGH SUMMER when this photograph of the Old Mill House was taken in the 1920s – note all the open windows.

THIS VENERABLE HOUSE was known as 'Fiddle' Botting's after its owner.

ANOTHER VIEW of 'Fiddle' Botting's in Franklynn Road taken further up the slope. From this viewpoint the spire of the Priory and the tower of St Wilfrid's are visible.

CLEAVE WATER FARM was situated just beyond the Fox and Hounds and this view dates from around 1907. The farm was run by E.L. Mills and high class butter, double cream and new laid eggs could be delivered twice daily.

SOUTHLANDS FARM photographed in around 1910. The farm used to stand north of Sydney Road near Church Avenue.

AN OLD VIEW OF AN OLD HOUSE at Tylers Green between Haywards Heath and Cuckfield.

KNOWN AS CANTON COTTAGE this house stood on the corner of Haywards Road and South Road. The beautiful shell decorations were done by the owner, Richard Shearlock, an ex-naval man.

BOLNORE was once the name of an old farmhouse, but this palatial Bolnore was designed by Decimus Burton for the Dealty family. It was a Miss Dealty who laid the foundation stone of St Wilfrid's Church.

ANOTHER VIEW of Bolnore set amongst its trees.

A WONDERFULLY CLEAR STUDY of Elfinsward by F. Douglas Miller. Note the croquet lawn. Elfinsward was a gift to the Diocese of Chichester from Mrs Gerald Moor and was opened by Bishop L.H. Burrows in 1928.

ELFINSWARD served as a conference centre and, as can be seen from this view, it had its own canteen. Elfinsward was sold in 1973 and later demolished.

THE SERGISON ARMS is Hayward Heath's oldest pub and was once called the Dolphin. This photograph was taken in around 1905 when John Barnes was the proprietor. The billboard advertises a function at the Public Hall.

THE SERGISON ARMS in another view, with a cart containing a milk churn drawn up before the entrance.

THE FOX AND HOUNDS INN, Wivelsfield Road, in around 1906 when it boasted good stabling and two lock-up coach houses. In 1861 the landlord was also a farmer with 24 acres of land to his name.

King Edward VII Memorial Eliot Cottage Hospital, Hayward...

THE HOSPITAL was opened in November 1912 by Princess Christian of Schleswig-Holstein. The matron was Miss M. Barrett and there were 12 beds in 4 wards.

The Bathing Pool, Birch Hotel, Haywards Heath

THE SWIMMING POOL at the Birch Hotel was beautifully sited with a wide prospect over the countryside. It was used by local residents as well as visitors. This view dates from the 1930s.

SECTION FOUR

Parks, Greens and Leafy Lanes

The Green. Haywards Heath

MUSTER GREEN itself is ancient, although the trees here on the left are young. It is marked on a manorial map of 1638.

A PEACEFUL VIEW of Muster Green with two sedate bicyclists.

MUSTER GREEN, with the road providing ample evidence that horse transport was still very much in use.

MUSTER GREEN, HAYWARDS HEATH.

IN THIS VIEW Muster Green has changed considerably. The thin footpath on the left has broadened, the mature trees have been pruned, there are poles carrying electricity or telegraph wires, the war memorial has been erected and there are two motor cars.

THE RECREATION GROUND was bought in 1887 for £384 to commemorate Queen Victoria's Golden Jubilee.

Entrance to Recreation Ground, Hayward's Heath.

THE RECREATION GROUND contains part of the original Heath. These two girls have their hoops with them. The card was posted in 1913.

THE CRICKET PAVILION in the Recreation Ground was opened on 12 September 1900.

THE CRICKET PAVILION decorated for Edward VII's coronation in August 1902.

QUEEN VICTORIA'S DIAMOND JUBILEE in 1897 was celebrated at Haywards Heath by the purchase of Pannett's meadow for £3,000 which then became Victoria Park. This lovely view dates from around 1913.

A WIDE VIEW OF VICTORIA PARK reminiscent of the time when it used to be Richard Pannett's meadow.

THE TREE-COVERED HILLOCK on the west side of the park was artificially created from earth thrown up when the nearby railway cutting was excavated.

AMERICA LANE owes its name to the Quaker benefactor, William Allen. He provided parcels of land with cottages for poor labourers and so the area was nicknamed the Colony and later America.

ANOTHER VIEW OF AMERICA LANE dating from around 1913. The original postcard is brightly coloured and the scene looks like the Fall in New England.

LUCASTES AVENUE was named after an ancient house in the area. The avenue must surely have been one of the leafiest roads in Haywards Heath.

A SUMMER VIEW OF ASHENGROUND BRIDGE with the lady appearing to be somewhat weighed down by her hat trimmings.

Ashenground Bridge, Haywards Heath

THE ASHENGROUND BRIDGE leads over the railway.

Scrase Bridge,   Hayward's Heath.

SCRASE BRIDGE was at one time at the northern extremity of the Heath belonging to Haywards Heath.

THE MEN WHO LEVELLED ROCKY LANE must have had a hard time of it. No wonder the name stuck.

THIS PART OF THE ROAD to Ardingly is known as High Beeches. Like Rocky Lane, it too features a sandstone outcrop. The view was taken by that well-known Haywards Heath photographer F. Douglas Miller.

Churches

Parish Church, Haywards Heath

ST WILFRID'S CHURCH was designed by G.F. Bodley and consecrated on Whit Monday 1965.

THE SITE NOW OCCUPIED BY THE CHURCHYARD was once part of the brickfield. The Lychgate was dedicated on Ascension Day 1909.

THIS IRON-CONSTRUCTED CHURCH used to stand in Sydney Road and it cost £900, of which Miss Otter donated £400. It was replaced by St Richard's.

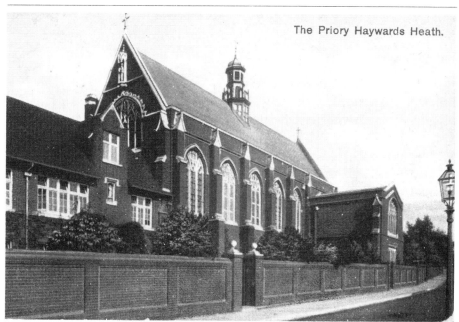

THE MAGNIFICENT CHAPEL belonging to the Priory of Our Lady of Good Counsel was designed by Edward Goldie and built in 1890. The Priory closed in 1977. ·

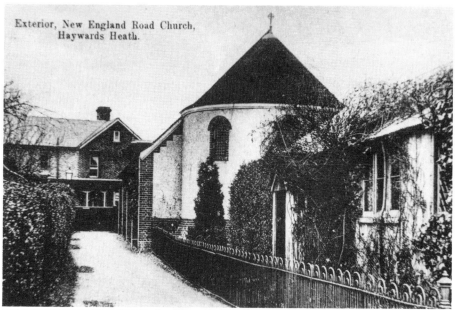

THE FULL TITLE OF THIS EDIFICE is the Church of the Presentation of Christ in the Temple. It was given by Mrs Mary Otter.

THE OPENING of the Congregational Church in South Street on 21 July 1915.

People

A RARE AND INTERESTING PHOTOGRAPH taken in 1899 and showing a fussy Victorian interior complete with peacock's feather and large fan in the fireplace. The little girl is Grace Uridge whose father ran the grocer's shop in Sussex Square. She was photographed in the rooms above the shop and she had to use a stool, perched on top of a chair, in order to reach the mirror.

THREE GENERATIONS AT ALVERSTOKE, Lucastes Avenue in about 1928. Alec Whitcher (on the right) became managing director of the Haywards Heath Gas Company in 1936.

JUDY SHARP photographed in around 1943 by Eva Pannell of no. 9 Boltro Road. The dress is white spotted muslin with smocking across the bodice and sleeves.

CAPTAIN SHARP of the Royal Sussex Regiment on leave in June 1943 with his wife Jean and children Judy and Nicholas at Alverstoke, Lucastes Avenue.

HAYWARDS HEATH BORN MARJORIE HALL was photographed by L.A. Wood of the Broadway Studios in 1942 wearing her Naafi uniform.

ST WILFRID'S GUIDE COMPANY. Back row, left to right: -?-, Rose Winslade, Gladys Thompsett, Dorothy Jeffery, Dorothy Margetts, Maud Daniels, Margaret Nunns. Middle row, left to right: Kathleen Welling, Edie Welling, Bessie Franks, Nora Stevens, Rene Burgess, Gladys Welling, Doris McBean, Lily Carter. Front row, left to right: Evelyn Boxall, Dora Doughty, Miss A.M. Alderton, Miss M. Watton, Miss G. Everson, Nellie Gurr, Violet Winslade.

THE STAFF OF THE THERMOGENE FACTORY on an outing in August 1919. Thermogene was a popular remedy for rheumatism and bronchitis. There were also factories in France, Germany and Belgium.

THE 1ST HAYWARDS HEATH COMPANY of Boys' Life Brigade in around 1920. Note the variety of jackets and collars and ties.

THE STAFF OF BEENY'S EMPORIUM photographed in fancy dress in the 1920s. The stout lady in the centre has 'Buy it at Beeny's on her apron.

THE HAYWARDS HEATH FIRE BRIGADE taking part in a competition, which they won, at Seaford in 1948. From left to right: Dick Barton, Sub-Officer Ayres, Leading Fireman Major Vidler, Fred Weller, Jack Thorne, Chief Fire Officer Thomas and Chief Fire Officer Mees.

Events

HAYWARDS HEATH'S first motor bus, photographed outside the Liverpool Arms in 1905 by F. Douglas Miller.

Telephone Disaster, Haywards Heath, January 8th 1908.

THERE WAS A BLIZZARD in January 1908 followed by a violent wind. The wires, already sagging under the weight of ice and snow, were brought crashing down by the strong wind. It caused havoc to the communications between Brighton and London as all 10 trunk lines through Haywards Heath and Wivelsfield were affected.

AFTER THE DISASTER Post Office officials gave notice that telephone calls to London would take over three hours to get through. It was stated that one and a half miles of wire had collapsed into the streets of Haywards Heath.

THE AVIATION PIONEER GORDON ENGLAND lived at Oakwood. In May 1911 P.H. Pixton, a fellow enthusiast, dropped by for a visit.

MORISON'S BIPLANE WRECKED AT OAKWOOD, HAYWARDS HEATH. MAY 9-1911
PHOTO A. SMITH H H

A DRAMATIC SHOT showing where Oscar Morison's biplane landed on 9 May 1911. Note the ladder on the right.

THE SCENE AT HAYWARDS HEATH on 22 June 1911, the day King George V and Queen Mary were crowned. Apparently it poured with rain.

THE EXPEDITIONARY FORCE marching to Newhaven in early 1914. The story goes that they marched through Haywards Heath once, discovered they had taken the wrong road, marched through the centre again and this time took the right road.

THE HAILSHAM BAND taking part in the Band Contest held at Haywards Heath on 1 June 1914.

THE MAY DAY PARADE, including a brass band and the firemen, appears to be led by a man pushing a pram. The banner belongs to Court Forester's Retreat (No. 4461 AOF).

THE CORN STORES next to the old railway station entrance in Market Place went up in flames on 21 October 1915.

AN ATMOSPHERIC PHOTOGRAPH taken by F. Douglas Miller of the Tradesmen's Cricket Tea.

MR GRIFFIN'S TUG-OF-WAR TEAM with their shirt sleeves rolled up for action.

A SUNLIT SCENE on 16 July 1935 as the children's playground on the St Clair meadow is declared open.

Schools

THE ORIGINAL SITE OF ST WILFRID'S SCHOOL, close to the church. The school opened in 1857. The notice in front of the trees reads 'Caution Motorists'.

A CLASS AT ST WILFRID'S SCHOOL in October 1914. The teacher is Mrs Purvey.

THE CHILDREN OF ST WILFRID'S SCHOOL celebrate May Day in around 1909.

THE NEW ST WILFRID'S SCHOOL was built in Eastern Road. It was officially opened on 27 April 1951 by the Bishop of Chichester, Dr G.K.A. Bell. The Revd H.H. Tarrant, vicar of St Wilfrid's from 1945 until 1957, stands to the right of the Bishop, while the tall man to the left is the Headmaster, Mr King.

THE CHILDREN OF ST WILFRID'S SCHOOL pictured with their May Day posies in 1956. The flowers were gathered by the children and later the posies were sent to the children of St John's, Carlton Hill, Brighton.

THESE NEATLY DRESSED GIRLS at the Holy Cross Convent were most probably orphans.

A SCENE IN THE GARDENS of the Priory in around 1912 which includes one of the nuns and some girls in their plaid uniform.

THE COUNCIL SCHOOLS (with separate entrances for boys and girls) in South Road in 1930. The schools opened in September 1907 and were enlarged in 1911. The site is now covered with shops.

FARLINGTON HOUSE, a private girls' school, was founded in 1896. The school grounds covered 12 acres in Oathall Road.

AT FARLINGTON there were five grass tennis courts and one hard court.

FARLINGTON'S GYMNASIUM in the 1940s.

A DORMITORY AT FARLINGTON in the 1940s. This was one of the show bedrooms; that is one of the two which were always shown to parents who might send their daughters to the school.

ANNE DYKES AND ALYS MITCHELL at Farlington in 1953. The shorts were a most uncomfortable garment.

A CLOSE UP of part of the 1951 Farlington school photograph. The teaching staff from right to left are: Mr Kay (Mathematics), Mademoiselle Ashemashare (French), Miss Dean (English Literature), Miss Bengough (Music), Miss E. Simpson (Headmistress 1942–1971), Miss Corfield (Elocution) with her dog Dwina, Miss Taylor (Music), Miss Crask, Matron and Sister (Miss Evans).

FARLINGTON was well-known for its theatrical productions. This photograph shows the cast of *I Have Five Daughters* produced in 1952. Standing left to right: Anne Dykes, Nina Horne, Jill Hyem, Rosemary Close, Jennifer Alderson-Smith, Jane Osmaston and Ann Campbell. Seated: Felicity Amor, Caroline Roberts, Susan Forsyth, Penelope Stephens, Angela Thorne, Gillian Charlesworth and Dione de Courcy.

ANOTHER FARLINGTON PRODUCTION of the 1950s was *Mary Rose* by J.M. Barrie. From left to right: Jane Greenhough, Elizabeth Castle and Felicity Amor.

FARLINGTON OLD GIRLS' DAY 30 June 1956. On the left stands the former Head Girl, Jill Hyem, now a successful film and television writer whose best known series are *Tenko* and *Wish Me Luck*. Standing on the right is Angela Thorne, now a well-known actress, one of whose most popular television roles is in *Three Up, Two Down*.

FARLINGTON GIRLS watching a partial eclipse of the sun through smoked glass in 1954.

TREVELYAN was another of Haywards Heath's many private schools, again for girls. This photograph shows the front entrance in around 1912. The school closed in 1966 and the building has been demolished.

THE GYMNASIUM AT TREVELYAN. The girl on the parallel bars is in danger of showing her stocking tops!

THE SCHOOLROOM AT TREVELYAN, when the joint principals were Miss Rolfe and Miss Kelsey.

A TREVELYAN DORMITORY in around 1912. Note the wash-stand sets and the curtains to provide separate cubicles.

BRUNSWICK WAS A BOYS' PREPARATORY SCHOOL situated next to Farlington. The photograph shows the Brunswick 1st XI cricket team of 1947. Back row, left to right: Sharp, Jackson, Ledger, Jones, Ghods and Stuart. Middle row: Roberts-Wray, King and Hawkins. Front row: Christiani and Wyatt. (Boys were known by their surnames alone).

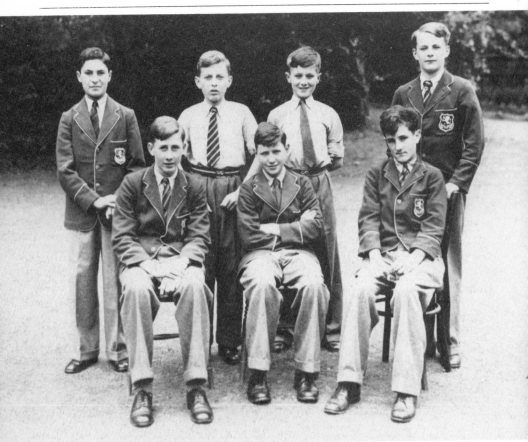

A GROUP OF BRUNSWICK PREFECTS in around 1948. Back row, left to right: Ghods, Wyatt, -?-, Collingwood. Front row: Hawkins, Stuart and Sharp.

SECTION NINE

St Francis Hospital

A POSTCARD showing the full Victorian splendour of the Hospital, designed by H.E. Kendall and opened in 1859. The photograph was taken in around 1925 and since then the Lodge on the left and the tall chimney have been demolished and the gate piers removed.

A GROUP OF TWO HOSPITAL GARDENERS (wearing cloth caps) and four nursing attendants in their uniforms and peaked caps in the 1920s. Harry Cooke stands in the back row, third from left. At a hospital reunion in 1976 Harry Cooke won a prize for being the oldest ex-member of staff present (he was in his nineties). The prize was a two-litre bottle of whisky.

THE HOSPITAL CRICKET TEAM in 1925. At that time the institution was called the Brighton Mental Hospital. Back row, left to right: F. Keeling, E. Doughty (Umpire) C.H. Morton, A. Colbran, C. Brownie (Scorer), F. Sparks, L. Room, M. Waterer (Hon Secretary). Middle row: G. Mason, A. Castle (Vice-Captain), W. Mitchell, (Captain), Dr Murphy, E.C. Newnham. Front row: W. Murrell, H. Hopps.

THE HOSPITAL FIRE BRIGADE in 1925. All male personnel had to receive training in fire fighting. Front row, from left to right: -?-, -?-, Mr F. Keeling, Dr Guppy, Chief Engineer Rees, Mr George Hastie Harper-Smith (Superintendent 1923–1938), Deputy Chief Engineer A. Castle, Dr Humphreys, Mr Weller (Deputy Chief Male Nurse).

A GROUP OF NURSES in 1931. Left to right: Nurse Wright (later Mrs Bellchambers), Nurse Brown (later Mrs Cox) and Sister Paul.

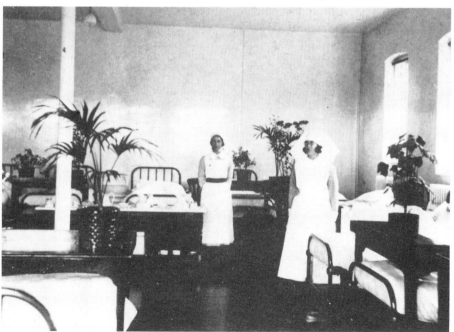

FEMALE WARD NINE in around 1932 with Sister Shelley and Staff Nurse Benjamin.

THE HOSPITAL ORCHESTRA outside the old Recreation Hall in around 1934. Back row, left to right: Dr Humphreys; -?-; -?-; Mr Fuller, double-bass; Mr Robson, piano; -?-. Second row: -?-, -?-, Mr Critchell, saxophone (nursing staff); Dr F.H. Guppy; Mr George Hastie Harper-Smith (Superintendent); Mr Knight (Bandmaster); Mr Herbert, violin and saxophone (Leader) and Mr Bolton, violin.

A WELL ATTENDED STAFF DANCE in February 1938 captured by W. Marchant of Lindfield.

THE RETIREMENT of the Matron, Miss J. Gordon, and the Superintendent, Mr George Hastie Harper-Smith, in 1938. Matron's faithful dog is in attendance too.

THE HOSPITAL BAND playing for the Coronation Staff Ball in 1953. Left to right: Ron Cheney (student nurse); Harry Barnett, accordion; Tom Brunton, drums (clerical staff); Fred Weller, violin (hospital electrician); -?-, pianist; Peter Woolwin, double-bass (hospital painter); Nick Carter, saxophone (head porter); Chris Gibbs, trombone (Harry Barnett's Band). Harry Barnett began training at St Francis in 1939 and apart from war service in the RAMC he spent his nursing career at St Francis and is the last Hospital Bandmaster.

SECTION TEN

The Railway

ywards Heath Station, Sussex.

A WOMAN LOOKS OUT of the window of her third class compartment as another train approaches. Note the mail-bags and post-boy. The postcard is franked Haywards Heath, 8.45 p.m., 8 August 1907.

THE ALL IMPORTANT RAILWAY to which Haywards Heath owes much of its prosperity, viewed from Rocky Lane Bridge.

HAYWARDS HEATH STATION as it appeared in 1898.

A FASCINATING VIEW from the Broadway in around 1908. Note the chicken runs in the foreground and the railway station, sidings and signal box on the left.

THIS VIEW was still being sent through the post in the 1940s, although it was actually taken in around 1930, before electrification arrived and the entrance to the railway station was still in its previous position in Market Place.

BURGESS HILL STATION photographed in around 1904.

A VIEW OF THE RAILWAY when steam was still king. Electric trains made their début on the Brighton line in 1932.

Wivelsfield Station, Sussex (showing the Through Manchester to Eastbourne Train coming from London).

AN EARLY VIEW of Wivelsfield Station which, apart from the station master and the approaching train, appears to be deserted.

Wivelsfield Junction, near Burgess Hill, Sussex

WIVELSFIELD JUNCTION in around 1905. Note the signalman on duty in his box, the two trains on the track to the right and the bridge over the line to the left.

A SUPERB VIEW of the Balcombe viaduct taken in around 1914 by F. Douglas Miller.

Entrance Ardingly Station, L. B. & S. C. Railway.

ARDINGLY STATION in around 1912 – a marvellously eccentric creation.

Burgess Hill

A CLEAR PHOTOGRAPH of the Burgess Hill Inn from around 1905, when Thomas Lacey was the proprietor.

THIS IMPOSING PHOTOGRAPH of a villa called The Lawns in Keymer Road was taken in the 1880s. It shows the family of Henry Johnson who ran the Keymer Brick Works. By 1931 the house had become known as The Croft and it was purchased by the Parents' National Educational Union to become the new Senior School.

THE MAGNIFICENT NEW POST OFFICE was opened in September 1906.

THE BURGESS HILL CARNIVAL on 24 July 1907. Perhaps they are Boer War veterans standing under the banner 'For King and Country'.

The Lake, Victoria Gardens, Burgess Hill

THE VICTORIA PLEASURE GARDENS were opened in 1898. There was a switchback railway (seen on the left), boating on the lake in the summer and, if the weather was cold enough, skating in the winter.

A VIEW OF THE SWINGS in Victoria Gardens with the switchback railway on the right.

ALL SAINTS OUTING   BURGESS HILL·1912·

(15) WILES HOVE

A GROUP OF HAPPY CHILDREN from All Saints Church, Hove, visit the Victoria Gardens in 1912. They are accompanied by the vicar of Hove who was also Bishop of Lewes, the Right Revd L.H. Burrows. He was considered something of a heart-throb by the ladies who avidly collected postcards in which he featured.

"Oh, listen to the Band."

at Victoria Gdns.
Burgess Hill
"Oh, Johnnie, we have missed u."
"Jack in the box."

THIS POSTCARD, dating back to around 1906, must have held fond memories for someone.

THE CINDER PATH, BURGESS HILL

TWO WORKMEN pause from their work tidying up the cinder path. The original postcard is printed in sepia tones.

CHURCH ROAD, Burgess Hill, photographed in around 1907. Mr Hole appears to have parked his car on the pavement outside his shop.

A CHARABANC EXCURSION pauses outside the King's Head, St John's Common in July 1916.

New Close Hill, Burgess Hill, Sussex.

AT FIRST GLANCE it looks as though an unfortunate man is hanging upside down, closer inspection reveals it is only his reflection.

THIS PHOTOGRAPH was taken in Burgess Hill on 3 October 1917 by W.G. Wheatley and shows Ernest Hole, engineer and millwright, with his workforce. Ernest Hole stands on the right wearing a bowler hat, while his son Edwin is the boy in the centre with an Eton collar. Edwin Hole was to continue working with the firm until his death at the age of 82 in 1988. The firm is now managed by Ernest Hole's grandson, Mr Tony Hole.

THE KEYMER BRICK AND TILE COMPANY WORKS in around 1938.

BURNT CLAY TILES being 'drawn' from a kiln in the Keymer Works in the 1960s. This kiln has since been demolished.

THE 2ND BURGESS HILL GUIDE COMPANY in 1919. The group was started by the PNEU School.

ARTHUR GEORGE GATES, a farmer, photographed in around 1902 with his wife Emma and their children outside North Black House, Burgess Hill. From left to right the children are: Geoffrey and Arthur (who both became school teachers), Kenneth (who became an organ builder) and Emma (also a teacher). The small children are Charlie (who later emigrated to Australia) and Evelyn.

TAKING AFTERNOON TEA in the garden of the Sperring's house in Jane's Lane in around 1928. Left to right: Dorothy Jackson, her mother Evelyn Jackson and her grandmother Emma Gates seated far right. Miss Ada Sperring is standing and Miss Ethel Sperring is seated.

JEAN WHITCHER photographed in around 1917 by Walter Cordrey of Burgess Hill. At the time her father Alec Whitcher was manager of the Burgess Hill Gas Co.

MISS WINIFRED CHEESMAN ran a small private school at her house, no. 231 Junction Road. This photograph was taken in around 1936. Back row, left to right: Joyce Green, Doreen Green, Barbara King, Lettie Moon, Dorothy Jackson. Middle row: Betty Grover, Miss Cheesman, Norma Nye, Daphne Berry. Front row: Alfred Moon, Eileen Costick, Margaret Jackson, Dennis Berry, Peggy Baker, Bobby Grover.

THE BURGESS HILL SCHOOL FOR GIRLS started life in a rented upstairs room in Church Road Chambers. There were nine children and their teacher was Miss Beatrice Goode from the PNEU headquarters at Ambleside.

The Gymnasium.

THE GYMNASIUM of the PNEU School was opened in 1932. Although intended as a temporary building, it was in use for 50 years.

Dalegarth.

DALEGARTH was used for many years as a boarding house for senior girls at the PNEU School. During the Second World War evacuated families lived there. It has now been demolished.

Thornhurst - Junior Boarding House.

THORNHURST is still part of the Burgess Hill School for Girls (but the ivy has gone). In the 1950s its name was changed to Silverdale East.

THIS TRANQUIL SPOT was once part of the gardens belonging to the PNEU School.

STANDARD ONE of the London Road Infants' School in around 1930. Note the abacus on the left and the favourite print on the wall of *The Boyhood of Raleigh* by Millais.

CHURCH ROAD pictured in the 1930s. Note the low slung pram outside Whitehouse's shop.

SECTION TWELVE

Cuckfield

THIS IS HOW THE HIGH STREET LOOKED in around 1905. The ivy-covered building on the right is the Talbot Hotel.

THE HIGH STREET, looking north in 1901. The dry summer scene contrasts strongly with the muddy winter one of the previous view.

A VIEW OF SOME OLD HOUSES in the High Street taken in 1907.

MR COOK at the door of his shop at No. 30 South Street, Cuckfield, in around 1910. Before he became a confectioner, his trade was bird stuffing.

A PHOTOGRAPH BY F. DOUGLAS MILLER of the frozen waterfall in Cuckfield Park.

THE OLD COTTAGES facing the churchyard of Holy Trinity photographed in 1907. The ivy-clad chimney is surely a monument to Victorian taste.

Lindfield

A GREAT WELCOME HOME for the boys back from active service, reflected in Lindfield's pond.

A LIVELY SCENE outside the schools at Lindfield.

OLD PLACE photographed in around 1908. The house was built in around 1590 and there is an interesting later association with Charles Eamer Kempe, who lived there and designed so much of the Victorian stained glass still to be seen in Sussex.

RUINS OF EAST MASCALLS, LINDFIELD. 1880.

THIS POSTCARD was sent in 1904, although the photograph was taken in 1880 and shows the terrible devastation following a fire at East Mascalls, Lindfield.

THE FINCHES AT LINDFIELD remarkable in this view of around 1908 for being entirely smothered in ivy.

THE MOTOR MISSION about to conduct an open air service in Lindfield in around 1912.

A WONDERFULLY CLEAR PHOTOGRAPH taken in 1887 showing some barns at Lindfield by Bedales Hill.

HIGH STREET, Lindfield. The lady who purchased this postcard in 1923 bought three bunches of deep pink sweet peas for 2d. each from the house whose blind is marked with an *x*.

Ditchling

THE HIGH STREET in around 1906 when an open or closed fly (a carriage) could be hired from the Bull Hotel. Note the stately perambulators on the left.

NORTH STREET, Ditchling, in around 1912.

LITTLE MISS WALLER, from an old Ditchling family, faces the camera in around 1899.

HAYMAKING at Ditchling in around 1904.

MR HOLMAN harvesting at North End Farm in the 1930s.

SHEPHERD REVELL with his flock at Ditchling in the 1920s.

LODGE HILL AND OLDLANDS MILL in around 1910.

EDWARD PHILIP ALFORD at East End Farm in 1931.

PETER ALFORD, son of E.P. Alford, at East End Farm in 1939.

MR BRANSTON, Ditchling Volunteer Fireman.

BOB MARSTON of the Ditchling Cricket Team in around 1916.

MABEL RUSSELL perched on the running-board of her Rolls Royce. She lived for many years at Ditchling and led a varied life, being once a Gaiety girl and later MP for Berwick-on-Tweed.

GUESTS AT MR STEYNING'S WEDDING in the 1920s stand outside the Ditchling Church Room (now gone).

THE DITCHLING FOOTBALL CLUB in 1930. Back row, left to right: J. Harwood, Martin Turner, G. Killick, G. Skinner, L. McKinnon, ? Adams. Front row: G. Thomas, D. Cottington, Frank Mayston, -?-, G. Pratt.

Hurstpierpoint and Hassocks

ANOTHER EVOCATIVE STUDY from the camera of F. Douglas Miller taken in around 1914 looking over Church Fields towards the church of Holy Trinity, Hurstpierpoint.

A QUIET CORNER at Hurstpierpoint with a house called The Odd Corner. It was photographed in the 1920s and the motor bike carries the registration number PM 1018.

THE CLAYTON PUMPING STATION in around 1900. It was owned by the Burgess Hill Water Company who also had pumping stations at Keymer and Ditchling.

Old Cottages, Hurstpierpoint. H.B.

OLD COTTAGES AT HURSTPIERPOINT; the ones on the right were demolished at around the turn of the century.

Entrance to the Village, Hurstpierpoint

A NOSTALGIC LOOK at a traditional farm waggon with the spire of Holy Trinity just visible in the background.

The Orchard Tea Gardens, Hassocks.

THIS POSTCARD was sent in 1911 and captures the popularity of the Orchard Tea Gardens at Hassocks.

F·S·ANNUAL FESTIVAL·HASSOCKS TEA GARDENS·MAY·17·1911 "A SEE·SAW OF BEAUTIES." (5) WILE NOV

A CHURCH OUTING to the Orchard Tea Gardens on 17 May 1911. The young ladies were accompanied by the Bishop's wife Mrs Burrows.

Keymer Road   Hassocks Sussex,

A DELIGHTFUL SCENE in Keymer Road, Hassocks. Is the man in the bowler hat the proud father of the children in the pony trap?

STONE POUND CROSS ROAD

THE STONE POUND CROSSROADS in around 1908. Note the old-fashioned finger-post and the board advertising the Friars Oak Hotel.

SECTION SIXTEEN

Ardingly and Balcombe

NOT MUCH DANGER in crossing this road at Ardingly.

Ardingly—Village Hall and Pump House

A VIEW OF ARDINGLY showing the attractive little pump house.

In Balcombe Forest.

THE POSITIONING OF THE TWO LADIES in this photograph by F. Douglas Miller emphasizes the huge girth of the tree trunks.

A POPULAR STYLE of genre postcard depicting the quaintness of country life at Balcombe.

ANOTHER POSTCARD of similar type. Note the village ancient in his smock looking like Old Father Time.

ACKNOWLEDGEMENTS

I should like to thank the following people and organisations for their help and for allowing me to use their photographs in this book:

Mr Harry Barnett • East Sussex County Library • Mrs Dorothy Gedye
Mr Tony Hole of Ernest Hole & Son Ltd., • Jill Hyem • Robert Jeeves of the
Picture Postcard Saloon • Mr Jones, Headmaster of St Wilfrid's School
Keymer Brick and Tile Co., • Mrs M. Nelson-Smith • Mr Philip Pye
Mrs Lilian Rogers • St Francis and Hurstwood Hospitals Museum Trust
Mr Seanor • Mr Nicholas Sharp • Miss Effie Simpson (former Farlington
Headmistress) • Mr and Mrs Jack Thorne • Mrs Barbara Webb, Headmistress
Burgess Hill School for Girls